The Black Box

Raising the standards of learning that are achieved through school education is an important national priority. Governments have been vigorous in the last ten years making changes in pursuit of this aim. National curriculum testing, the development of the GCSE, league tables of school performance, initiatives to improve school planning and management, target setting, more frequent and thorough inspection—these are all means to the end. But the sum of all of these doesn't add up to an effective policy, because something is missing.

Learning is driven by what teachers and pupils do in classrooms. Here, teachers have to manage complicated and demanding situations, channeling the personal, emotional, and social pressures among a group of 30 or so youngsters in order to help them learn now and become better learners in the future. Standards can only be raised if teachers tackle this task more effectively—what is missing from the policies is any direct help with this task.

In terms of systems engineering, present policy seems to treat the classroom as a *black box*. Certain *input* from the outside is fed in or makes demands—pupils, teachers, other resources, management rules and requirements, parental anxieties, tests with pressures to score highly, and so on. Some *output* follows, hopefully pupils who are more knowledgeable and competent, better test results, and teachers who are more or less satisfied and more or less exhausted. But what is happening inside? How can anyone be sure that a particular set of new input will produce better output if we don't at least study what happens inside?

The answer usually is that it is up to teachers—they have to make the inside work better. This answer is not good enough for two reasons. First, it is at least possible that some changes in the input may be counterproductive, making it harder for teachers to raise standards. Second, it seems strange, even unfair, to leave the most difficult piece of the standards-raising task entirely to teachers. If there are possible ways in which policy makers and others can give direct help and support to the everyday classroom task of achieving better learning, then surely these ways ought to be pursued vigorously.

None of the reform items mentioned in the first paragraph are aimed at direct help and support. To be sure, inspections do look inside classrooms, and insofar as they focus on what is happening there they draw attention to important issues. But they are not designed to give help and support, recommendations being in very general terms.

This booklet is about the inside of the black box. It is focused on one aspect of teaching—formative assessment—but the argument that we develop is that this feature is at the heart of effective teaching.

The Argument

We start from the self-evident proposition that teaching and learning have to be interactive. Teachers need to know about their pupils' progress and difficulties with learning so that they can adapt their work to meet pupils' needs—needs that are often unpredictable and vary from one pupil to another. Teachers can find out what they need in a variety of ways—from observation and discussion in the classroom and from written work of pupils, whether done as homework or in class.

In this paper, the term "assessment" refers to all those activities undertaken by teachers *and by their students in assessing themselves*, which provide information to be used as feedback to modify the teaching and learning activities in which they are engaged. *Such assessment becomes "formative" when the evidence is actually used to adapt the teaching work to meet the needs.*

There is nothing new about this. All teachers make assessments in every class they teach. But there are three important questions about this process that this paper sets out to answer. These are:

First: Is there evidence that improving formative assessment raises standards?

Second: Is there evidence of room for improvement?

Third: Is there evidence about how to improve formative assessment?

In setting out to answer these questions, we have conducted an extensive survey of the research literature. This has involved checking through many books and the issues of over 160 journals for the past nine years, and studying earlier reviews of research. This process yielded about 580 articles or chapters to study. Out of this, we have prepared a lengthy review, which uses material from 250 of these sources. The review is being published in the journal *Assessment in Education* (Black and Wiliam, 1998) together with comments on our work by leading educational experts from Australia, France, Hong Kong, Southern Africa, and the USA.

The conclusion we reached from the full review is that the answer to each of the above three questions is a clear "yes." The three main sections of this booklet will outline the nature and force of the evidence that justifies this conclusion. However, we are presenting a summary so that our text will appear strong on assertions and weak on the details of their justification. Our position is that these assertions are all backed by evidence and that this backing is set out in full detail in the lengthy review on which this booklet is based.

We believe that our three sections establish a strong case—that government, its agencies, and the teaching profession should study very carefully if they are seriously interested in raising standards in education. However, we also acknowledge widespread evidence that fundamental educational change can only be achieved slowly—through programs of professional development that build on existing good practice. So we are not concluding that, in formative assessment, we have yet another "magic bullet" for education. The issues involved are too complex and too closely linked to both the difficulties of classroom practice and the beliefs that drive public policy. In a fourth and final section, we confront this complexity and try to sketch out a strategy for acting on our evidence.

Is There Evidence That Improving Formative Assessment Raises Standards?

A review published in 1986, concentrating—but not exclusively—on classroom assessment work for children with mild handicaps, surveyed a large number of innovations, from which 23 were selected (Fuchs and Fuchs 1986). This group all satisfied the condition that quantitative evidence of learning gains was obtained, both for those involved in the innovation and for a similar group not so involved. Since then, many more papers have been published describing similarly careful quantitative experiments. Our own review has selected at least 20 more such studies—the number depends on how rigorous a set of selection criteria are applied. All of these studies show that innovations that include strengthening the practice of formative assessment produce significant, and often substantial, learning gains. These studies range over ages (from five-year-olds to university undergraduates), across several school subjects, and over several countries.

For research purposes, learning gains of this type are measured by comparing (a) the average improvements in pupils' scores on tests with (b) the range of scores that are found for typical groups of pupils on these same tests.

The ratio of (a) divided by (b) is known as the *effect size*. The formative assessment experiments produce typical effect sizes between 0.4 and 0.7: such effect sizes are larger than most of those found for educational interventions. The following examples illustrate some practical consequences of such large gains:

- An effect size of 0.4 would mean that the average pupil involved in an innovation would record the same achievement as a pupil just in the top 35 percent of those not so involved.
- A gain of effect size 0.4 would improve performances of pupils in GCSE by between one and two grades.
- A gain of effect size 0.7, if realized in the recent international comparative studies in mathematics (Beaton et al. 1996), would raise England from the middle of the 41 countries involved to being one of the top five.

Some of these studies exhibit another important feature. *Many of them show that improved formative assessment helps the (so-called) low attainers more than the rest and reduces the spread of attainment while also raising it overall.* One very recent study is entirely devoted to low-attaining students and students with learning disabilities and shows that frequent assessment feedback helps both groups enhance their learning (Fuchs et al. 1997). Any gains for such pupils could be particularly important, for any "tail" of low educational achievement is clearly a portent of wasted talent. Furthermore, pupils who come to see themselves as unable to learn usually cease to take school seriously—many of them will be disruptive within school, others will resort to truancy. Given the habits so developed, and the likelihood that they will leave school without adequate qualifications, such pupils are likely to be alienated from society and become the sources and victims of serious social problems.

So it seems clear that very significant learning gains could lie within our grasp. The fact that such gains have been achieved by a variety of methods which have, as a common feature, enhanced formative assessment, indicates that it is this feature which accounts, at least in part, for the successes. However, it does not follow that it would be an easy matter to achieve such gains on a wide scale in normal classrooms. The reports we have studied bring out, between and across them, other features that seem to characterize many of the studies, namely:

- All such work involves new ways to enhance feedback between those taught and the teacher, ways that require new modes of pedagogy, which will need significant changes in classroom practice.

- Underlying the various approaches are assumptions about what makes for effective learning—in particular that students have to be actively involved.
- For assessment to function formatively, the results have to be used to adjust teaching and learning—so a significant aspect of any program will be the ways in which teachers do this.
- The ways in which assessment can affect the motivation and self-esteem of pupils and the benefits of engaging pupils in self-assessment both deserve careful attention.

Is There Evidence of Room for Improvement?

A Poverty of Practice

There is a wealth of research evidence that the everyday practice of assessment in classrooms is beset with problems and shortcomings, as the following quotations indicate:

> "Marking is usually conscientious but often fails to offer guidance on how work can be improved. In a significant minority of cases, marking reinforces underachievement and under-expectation by being too generous or unfocused. Information about pupil performance received by the teacher is insufficiently used to inform subsequent work" *(OFSTED 1996)*.

> "Why is the extent and nature of formative assessment in science so impoverished?" *(UK secondary science teachers – Daws and Singh 1996)*.

> "The criteria used were 'virtually invalid by external standards'." *(Belgian primary teachers – Grisay 1991)*.

> "Indeed they pay lip service to it but consider that its practice is unrealistic in the present educational context" *(Canadian secondary teachers – Dassa, Vazquez-Abad, and Ajar 1993)*.

The most important difficulties, which are found in the UK but also elsewhere, may be briefly summarized in three groups. The first is concerned with *effective learning*:

- Teachers' tests encourage rote and superficial learning; this is seen even where teachers say they want to develop understanding—and many seem unaware of the inconsistency.
- The questions and other methods used are not discussed with or shared between teachers in the same school, and they are not critically reviewed in relation to what they actually assess.

- For primary teachers particularly, there is a tendency to emphasize quantity and presentation of work and to neglect its quality in relation to learning.

The second group is concerned with *negative impact*:

- The giving of marks and the grading functions are overemphasized, while the giving of useful advice and the learning function are underemphasized.
- Use of approaches in which pupils are compared with one another, the prime purpose of which appears to them to be competition rather than personal improvement. In consequence, assessment feedback teaches pupils with low attainments that they lack "ability," so they are not motivated, believing that they are unable to learn.

The third group focuses on the *managerial role* of assessments:

- Teachers' feedback to pupils often seems to serve social and managerial functions, often at the expense of the learning functions.
- Teachers are often able to predict pupils' results on external tests—because their own tests imitate them—but at the same time, they know too little about their pupils' learning needs.
- The collection of marks to fill up records is given greater priority than the analysis of pupils' work to discern learning needs; furthermore, some teachers pay no attention to the assessment records of previous teachers of their pupils.

Of course, not all of these descriptions apply to all classrooms, and indeed there will be many schools and classrooms to which they do not apply at all. Nevertheless, these general conclusions have all been drawn by authors in several countries, including the UK, who have collected evidence by observation, interviews, and questionnaires from many schools.

The Empty Commitment

The changes in England and Wales since the 1988 Education Reform Act have had powerful effects on assessment. The statements of policy which preceded that Act, the recommendations of the TGAT (Task Group on Assessment and Testing, DES 1988) report, and all subsequent statements of government policy have emphasized the importance of formative assessment by teachers. However, most of all available resources, and public and political attention, have been concentrated on tests that are given at the end of the Key Stages to yield overall levels or grades, and while teachers' contributions to these "summative" assessments have been given some formal status, hardly any attention is paid to them. Moreover, the problems of the relationship between teachers' formative and summative roles have received no attention.

There is indeed a very sharp contrast between these formal commitments to the central importance of formative assessment and the actual priority given to it. The clearest evidence of this is in the detailed account—written by one of its members—of the work of the Schools Examinations and Assessment Council (SEAC) between its foundation in 1988 and 1993 (Daugherty 1995). During that time, teachers' assessments appeared as an explicit item on that Council's agenda on only two occasions, each time because the government department (then the Department of Education and Science) had addressed a specific question about summative aspects, while the formative aspects of teachers' assessments were never given serious attention. Therefore, the body charged to carry out government policy on assessment had no strategy either to study or develop the formative assessment of teachers and did no more than devote a tiny fraction of its resources to publications concerned with such work.

The political commitment to external testing of teachers and schools in order to promote competition through league tables had a central priority, while the commitment to formative assessment was probably a marginal feature. As researchers the world over have found, external tests, such as the National Curriculum tests and the GCSEs, which function as high-stakes tests, always dominate both teaching and assessment. In particular, because of their constraints and function to provide overall summaries of achievement rather than helpful diagnoses, they give teachers poor models for formative assessment.

It is also possible that many of the commitments were stated in the belief that formative assessment was not problematic—that it already happened all the time and needed no more than formal acknowledgment of its existence. Some attempts were made, by the SEAC and subsequently by its successor, the School Curriculum and Assessment Authority (SCAA), to support teachers' assessments by producing general guides to procedures and publishing examples of pupils' work with guidance on how these concrete examples would be assessed. The general guides were not found to be helpful, and they could not be, given that they were not based on serious study of practical problems. The materials for exemplification have been valuable, but being guides to the interpretation of national curriculum criteria in the marking of pupils' work, they do not constitute a significant contribution to the development of formative work and indeed might enhance the summative rather than formative roles of teachers' assessment work.

Given this, it is hardly surprising that numerous research studies of the implementation of the UK's educational reforms have found that formative assessment is, as one put it, "seriously in need of development" (Russell et al. 1995). However, more recent research studies have found some improvement in formative practice in primary schools (Gipps et al. 1996), and over the past two years, the DfEE has allocated in-service GEST funds to the specific purpose of developing teacher assessment at Key Stage 2, and this has made it possible for some LEAs to begin to improve formative assessment through in-service training. Such developments are welcome, but as yet they do not begin to redress the effects of neglect and lost opportunities.

With hindsight, it can be seen that the failure to perceive the need for substantial support for formative assessment and take responsibility for developing such support was a serious error. Even in relation to the needs of the education system before 1988, formative assessment was weak. Given the new and mountainous burdens of the National Curriculum changes, it should have been clear that existing good practice could hardly have survived, let alone have risen to the challenge of a far more demanding set of requirements.

Is There Evidence About How to Improve Formative Assessment?

The Self-Esteem of Pupils

> " . . . a number of pupils . . . are content to 'get by' . . . . Every teacher who wants to practice formative assessment must reconstruct the teaching contracts so as to counteract the habits acquired by his pupils." *(Perrenoud, talking of pupils in Switzerland, 1991)*

The ultimate user of assessment information that is elicited in order to improve learning is the pupil. Here there are two aspects—one negative, one positive. The negative is illustrated by the above quotation. Where the classroom culture focuses on rewards, "gold stars," grades, or class rankings, pupils look for the ways to obtain the best marks rather than at the needs of their learning, which these marks ought to reflect. One reported consequence is that where they have any choice, pupils avoid difficult tasks. They also spend time and energy looking for clues to the "right answer." Many are reluctant to ask questions out of fear of failure. Pupils who encounter difficulties and poor results are led to believe that they lack ability, and this belief leads them to attribute their difficulties to a defect in themselves about which they cannot do a great deal. So they "retire hurt," avoid investing effort in learning that could only lead to disappointment, and try to build up their self-esteem in other ways. While the high achievers can do well in such a culture, the overall result is to enhance the frequency and extent of under-achievement.

The positive aspect is that such outcomes are not inevitable. What is needed is a culture of success backed by a belief that all can achieve. Formative assessment can be a powerful weapon here if it is communicated in the right way. While it can help all pupils, it gives particularly good results with low achievers, where it concentrates on specific problems with their work and gives them both a clear understanding of what is wrong and achievable targets for putting it right. Pupils can accept and work with such messages, provided that they are not clouded by overtones about ability, competition, and comparison with others. In summary, the message can be stated as follows:

Feedback to any pupil should be about the particular qualities of his or her work, with advice on what he or she can do to improve and avoid comparisons with other pupils.

Self-Assessment by Pupils

However, there is a further dimension. Many of the successful innovations have developed peer assessment and self-assessment by pupils as ways of enhancing formative assessment, and such work has achieved some success with pupils from age five upward. This link of formative assessment to self-assessment is not an accident—it is indeed inevitable.

To explain this, it should first be noted that the main problem those developing self-assessment encounter is not the problem of reliability and trustworthiness; it is found that pupils are generally honest and reliable in assessing both themselves and one another and can be too hard on themselves as often as they are too kind. The main problem is different—it is that pupils can assess themselves only when they have a sufficiently clear picture of the targets that their learning is meant to attain. Surprisingly, and sadly, many pupils do not have such a picture and appear to have become accustomed to receiving classroom teaching as an arbitrary sequence of exercises with no overarching rationale. It requires hard and sustained work to overcome this pattern of passive reception. When pupils do acquire such overview, they then become more committed and effective as learners: their own assessments become an object of discussion with their teachers and with one another, and this promotes even further that reflection on one's own ideas is essential to good learning.

What this amounts to is that self-assessment by pupils, far from being a luxury, is in fact an essential component of formative assessment. Where anyone is trying to learn, feedback about their efforts has three elements—the *desired goal*, the evidence about their *present position*, and some understanding of a *way to close the gap* between the two (Sadler 1989). All three must, to a degree, be understood by anyone before they can take action to improve their learning.

Such argument is consistent with more general ideas established by research into the way that people learn. New understandings are not simply swallowed and stored in isolation—they have to be assimilated in relation to preexisting ideas. The new and the old may be inconsistent or even in conflict, and the disparities have to be resolved by thoughtful actions taken by the learner. Realizing that there are new goals for learning is an essential part of this process.

For formative assessment to be productive, pupils should be trained in self-assessment so that they can understand the main purposes of their learning and thereby grasp what they need to do to achieve.

The Evolution of Effective Teaching

The research studies referred to in the first part of this booklet show very clearly that effective programs of formative assessment involve far more than the addition of a few observations and tests to an existing program. They require careful scrutiny of all of the main components of a teaching plan. As the argument develops, it becomes clear that instruction and formative assessment are indivisible.

To begin, the choice of tasks for class and homework is important. Tasks have to be justified in terms of the learning aims that they serve, and they can only work well if opportunities for pupils to communicate their evolving understanding are built into the planning. Discussion; observation of activities; and marking of written work can all be used to provide the opportunities, but it is then important to look at, or listen carefully to, the talk; the writing; and the actions through which pupils develop and display the state of their understanding.

Opportunities for pupils to express their understanding should be designed into any piece of teaching, for this will initiate the interaction whereby formative assessment aids learning.

Discussions in which pupils are led to talk about their understanding in their own ways are important aids to improve knowledge and understanding. Dialogue with the teacher provides the opportunity for the teacher to respond to and reorient the pupil's thinking. However, there are clearly recorded examples of such discussions where teachers have, quite unconsciously, responded in ways that would inhibit the future learning of a pupil. What the examples have in common is that the teacher is looking for a particular response and lacks the flexibility or confidence to deal with the unexpected. So the teacher tries to direct the pupil toward giving the expected answer. In maneuvering the conversation this way, the teacher seals off any unusual, often thoughtful but unorthodox, attempts by the pupils to work out their own answers. Over time the pupils get the message—they are not required to think out their own answers. The object of the exercise is to work out, or guess, what answer the teacher expects to see or hear and then express it so that the teaching can proceed.

A particular feature of the talk between teacher and pupils is the asking of questions by the teacher. This natural and direct way of checking on learning is often unproductive. One common problem is that teachers do not allow enough quiet time so that pupils can think and offer an answer. As often happens, a teacher answers her or his own question after only two or three seconds because a minute of pupils' silent thought is not tolerable, so there is no possibility that a pupil can think out what to say. There are then two consequences. One is, because the only questions that can produce answers in such a short time are questions of fact, these predominate. The other is that pupils don't even try to think about a response—if they know that the answer or another question will come along in a few seconds, there is no point in trying. It is also common that only a few pupils in a class answer the teacher's questions. The rest of the pupils then leave it to these few, knowing that they cannot respond as quickly and are unwilling to risk making mistakes in public. So the teacher, by lowering the level of questions and accepting answers from a few, can keep the lesson going but is actually out of touch with the understanding of most of the class—the question-answer dialogue becomes a ritual, one in which all connive, and thoughtful involvement suffers.

There are several ways to break this particular cycle. They involve giving pupils time to respond; asking them to discuss their thinking in pairs or small groups so that a respondent is speaking on behalf of others; giving pupils a choice between different possible answers and asking them to vote on the options; asking all to write down an answer and then reading out a selected few; and so on. What is essential is that any dialogue should evoke thoughtful reflection in which all pupils can be encouraged to take part, for only then can the formative process start to work.

The dialogue between pupils and a teacher should be thoughtful, reflective, focused to evoke and explore understanding, and conducted so that all pupils have an opportunity to think and express their ideas.

Class tests, and tests or other exercises set for homework, are also important means to promote feedback. A good test can be a learning as well as testing occasion. It is better to have frequent short tests than infrequent longer ones. Any new learning should first be tested within about a week of the first encounter, but tests more frequent than this are counterproductive. The quality of the test items (i.e., their relevance to the main learning aims and their clear communication to the pupil) needs scrutiny. Good questions are hard to generate, and teachers should collaborate and draw critically on outside sources to collect such questions.

Given questions of good quality, it is then essential to ensure the quality of the feedback. Research studies have shown that if pupils are given only marks or grades, they do not benefit from the feedback on their work. The worst scenario is one in which some pupils get low marks this time, they got low marks last time, they expect to get low marks next time, and this is accepted as part of a shared belief between them and their teacher that they are just not clever enough. Feedback has been shown to improve learning where it gives each pupil specific guidance on strengths and weaknesses, preferably without any overall marks. So, the way in which test results are reported back to pupils for them to identify their own strengths and weaknesses is a critical feature. Pupils must be given the means and opportunities to work with evidence of their difficulties. For formative purposes, a test at the end of a block or module of teaching is pointless in that it is too late to work with the results.

Tests and homework exercises can be an invaluable guide to learning, but the exercises must be clear and relevant to learning aims. The feedback on them should give each pupil guidance on how to improve, and each must be given opportunity and help to work at the improvement.

All these points make clear that there is no one simple way to improve formative assessment. What is common to them is that a teacher's approach should start by being realistic—confronting the question "Do I really know enough about the understanding of my pupils to be able to help each of them?"

Much of the work needed can give rise to difficulties. Some pupils will resist attempts to change accustomed routines, for any such change is threatening, and emphasis on the challenge to think for yourself (and not just work harder) can be disturbing to many. Pupils cannot be expected to believe in the value of changes for their learning before they have experienced the benefits of change.

Many of the initiatives that are needed take more class time, particularly when a central purpose is to change the outlook on learning and the working methods of pupils. Therefore, teachers have to take risks in the belief that such investment of time will yield rewards in the future, while "delivery" and "coverage" with poor understanding are pointless and even harmful.

Underlying such problems will be two basic issues. The one is the nature of *each teacher's beliefs about learning*. If the assumption is that knowledge is to be transmitted and learned, understanding will develop later, and clarity of exposition accompanied by rewards for patient reception are the essentials of good teaching, then formative assessment is hardly necessary. If, however, teachers accept the wealth of evidence that this transmission model does not work, even by its own criteria, then the commitment must be to teaching through interaction to develop each pupil's power to incorporate new facts and ideas into his or her understanding. Then formative assessment is an essential component—but one that is built in with other features that are also needed to secure the responsible and thoughtful involvement of all pupils. This is not meant to imply that individualized, one-on-one teaching is the only solution; rather, what is needed is a classroom culture of questioning and deep thinking in which pupils will learn from shared discussions with teachers and one another.

The other issue is the *beliefs that teachers hold about the potential of all of their pupils to learn*. To sharpen the contrast by overstating it, there is on the one hand the *fixed IQ* view—a belief that each pupil has a fixed, inherited intelligence, so that little can be done apart from accepting that some can learn quickly and others can hardly learn at all. On the other hand, there is the *untapped potential* view, prevalent in other cultures, which starts from the assumption that so-called "ability" is a complex of skills that can be learned. Here, the underlying belief is that all pupils can learn more effectively if one can clear away, by sensitive handling, the obstacles set up by previous difficulties, be they of cognitive failures never diagnosed, damage to personal confidence, or a combination of the two. Clearly the truth lies between these two extremes, *but the evidence is that ways of managing formative assessment that work with the assumptions of "untapped potential" do help all pupils learn and can give particular help to those who have previously fallen behind.*

Policy & Practice

Changing the Policy Perspective

The assumptions driving our national policy for assessment have been changing since 1988. Initially, it was promoted as an important component forestablishing the competitive market in education. This now has lower priority, with a shift toward emphasis on target setting for all, with assessment providing the touchstone to help check pupils' attainments. This is a more mature position, *but we would argue that there is a need now to move further, to focus on the inside of the "black box" and explore the potential of assessment to raise standards directly as an integral part of each pupil's learning work.*

It follows from this view that several changes are needed. First and foremost, policy ought to start with a recognition that the locus for raising standards is the classroom, so that the overarching priority has to be to promote and support change within the classroom. Attempts to raise standards by reform of the input and output to and from the black box of the classroom can be helpful, but they cannot be adequate on their own, and whether or not they are helpful can only be judged in the light of their effects in classrooms.

The evidence we have presented here establishes that a clearly productive way to start implementing a classroom-focused policy would be to improve formative assessment. This same evidence also establishes that to do this would not be to concentrate on some minor or idiosyncratic aspect of the whole business of teaching and learning. *Rather it would be concentrated on several essential elements, namely the quality of teacher-pupil interactions, the stimulus and help for pupils to take active responsibility for their own learning, the particular help needed to move pupils out of the "low-attainment" trap, and the development thereby of the habits needed by all if they are to become capable of lifelong learning.* Improvements in formative assessment that are within reach can contribute substantially to raising standards in all of these aspects.

Four Steps to Implementation

If the above argument is accepted, then what needs to be done? Here, of course, we have to go beyond the evidence about assessment and call on more general sources for guidance (Black and Atkin 1996; Fullan 1991).

At one extreme, one might call for more research to find out how best to carry out such work, and the other extreme could call for an immediate and large-scale program, with new guides, perhaps even rules, that all teachers should put into practice. Neither of these alternatives is sensible—the apparent paradox is that while the first is unnecessary because enough is known from the results of research, the second would be unjustified because not enough is known about classroom practicalities within the context of this country's schools.

The improvement of formative assessment cannot be a simple matter. There is no "quick fix" that can be added to existing practice with promise of rapid reward. On the contrary, if the substantial rewards of which the evidence holds out promise are to be secured, this will only come about if each teacher finds his or her own ways of incorporating the lessons and ideas that are set out above into his or her own patterns of classroom work. This can only happen relatively slowly and through sustained programs of professional development and support. This does not weaken the message here—indeed, it should be a sign of its authenticity, for lasting and fundamental improvements in teaching and learning can only happen this way. A recent international study of innovation and change in education encompassing 23 projects in 13 member countries of the OECD has arrived at exactly the same message in framing advice to the member countries about effective policies for change (Black and Atkin 1996).

Such arguments lead us to propose a four-point scheme for development, as follows.

1. Learning from development

Teachers will not take up attractive-sounding ideas, albeit based on extensive research, if these are presented as general principles that leave entirely to them the task of translating them into everyday practice—their classroom lives are too busy and fragile for this to be possible for all but an outstanding few. What they need is a variety of living examples of implementation—by teachers with whom they can identify and from whom they can derive both conviction and confidence that they can do better—and see concrete examples of what doing better means in practice.

So the program development cannot start with an extensive program of training for all—that could only be justified if it could be claimed that there exists enough "trainers" who know what to do, which is not the case. The essential first step is to set up a small number of local groups of schools (some primary, secondary, inner city, from suburban, and rural) with each committed both to a school-based development of formative assessment and collaboration within their local group. In such a process, the teachers in their classrooms will be working out the answers to many of the practical questions that the evidence presented here cannot answer and reformulating the issues, perhaps in relation to fundamental insights and certainly in terms that can make sense to their peers in ordinary classrooms. It would also be essential to carry out such development in a range of subject areas—the research reports of those developing mathematics education are significantly different from those in language and different again from those working in the creative arts (to quote only three examples). The schools involved would need extra support, to give their teachers time to plan the initiative in the light of existing evidence, reflect on their experience as it develops, and advise on training work for others in the future. In addition, there would be a need to support external evaluators to work with the teachers to help their development of the work and collect evidence about its effectiveness. Such evidence would both help guide policy implementation and disseminate findings to others. Video studies of classroom work would be an essential component for this latter purpose.

2. Dissemination

This dimension of the implementation would be low key at the outset—giving no more than general encouragement with explanation of some of the relevant evidence that schools might consider in light of their existing practices. It would become more proactive when results and resources became available from the development program. Then strategies for wider dissemination would have to be pursued, for example through earmarking of funding for relevant in-service programs.

It has to be emphasized that this will inevitably be a slow development. *To repeat what was said above, if the substantial rewards of which the evidence holds out promise are to be secured, this will only come about if each teacher finds his or her own ways of incorporating the lessons and ideas that are set out above into his or her own patterns of classroom work.* Even with optimum training and support, this will take time.

3. Reducing obstacles

> "Most of the teachers in this study were caught in conflicts among belief systems, institutional structures, agendas, and values. The point of friction among these conflicts was assessment, which was associated with very powerful feelings of being overwhelmed, and of insecurity, guilt, frustration, and anger ... . This study suggests that assessment, as it occurs in schools, is far from a mere technical problem. Rather, it is deeply social and personal."
>
> *(US secondary language teachers—Johnston* et al. *1995)*

All features in the educational system that actually obstruct the development of effective formative assessment should be examined to see how their negative effects can be reduced. The outstanding influence here is that of short external tests. Such tests can dominate teachers' work, and insofar as they encourage drilling to produce right answers to short, out-of-context questions, this dominance can draw teachers away from the paths to effective formative work. They can thereby constrain teachers to act against their own better judgment about the best ways to develop the learning of their pupils. This is not to argue that all such tests are unhelpful, and indeed they have an important role to play in securing public confidence in the accountability of schools. For the immediate future, what is needed is that in the evaluation of such tests—and in any development program for formative assessment—the interactions between the two should be studied with care to see how the models of assessment that external tests can provide could be made more helpful.

All teachers have to undertake some summative assessment, for example to report to parents, and to produce end-of-year reports as classes are due to move on to new teachers. However, the task of assessing pupils summatively for external purposes is clearly different from the task of assessing ongoing work to monitor and improve progress. Some argue that these two roles are so different that they should be kept apart. We do not see how this can be done, given that teachers must have some share in responsibility for the former and must take the leading responsibility for the latter. Indeed, from the information that teachers gather for formative purposes, they should, with selection and reinterpretation, be in a strong position to contribute to a fair summative report on each pupil (Wiliam and Black 1996). However, there are clearly difficult problems for teachers in reconciling their formative with their summative roles, and it is also evident from several evaluation studies of teachers' assessment practices in the UK in recent years that confusion in teachers' minds between the roles has impeded progress.

The role of teachers' assessment in GCSE and A-level examinations is a particular issue here. John Major's thoughtless intervention in 1991 (quoted in Daugherty 1995), when he declared that the contribution of teachers' assessments of coursework to public examination results should be reduced, limited this role and so set back the very substantial progress made over many years in developing the procedures to enhance the quality of such contributions. If that setback could be reversed and new priority given to solving the problems attendant on such contributions, this could be helpful in enhancing and giving impetus to the development of assessment skills by teachers. More significantly, it could raise the status of teachers' assessments and help them in resolving what the above quotation refers to as the "deeply social and personal" problems that many teachers have about their roles in assessment.

As already pointed out, enhancing the quality of learning through improved formative feedback takes classroom time and is in conflict where teachers feel under pressure to cover a statutory curriculum. An important contribution here would be a reduction in the content of that curriculum when it is revised for the year 2000.

4. Research

It is not difficult to set out a list of research questions that would justify further research in this area. The underlying reason for this is that, despite the many and varied reports of successful innovations, they fail to give clear accounts on one or other of the important details, for example about the actual classroom methods used, the motivation and experience of the teachers, the nature of the tests used as measures of success, or the outlooks and expectations of the pupils involved.

However, while there is ample justification for proceeding with carefully formulated projects, we do not judge that everything should wait on these. Enough is known to provide a basis for active development work, and some of the most important questions can be answered only in a program of practical implementation.

Examples of research questions for the future could be a study of the ways in which teachers understand and deal with the relationship between their formative and summative roles or a comparative study of the predictive validity of teachers' summative assessments compared with external test results. Many more examples could be formulated, and it would be important for future development that some of the many problems should be tackled by basic research. At the same time, experienced researchers would also have a vital role to play in the evaluation of the development programs proposed above.

Are We Serious About Raising Standards?

We believe our findings should be studied immediately by a variety of responsible agencies, such as the new Qualifications and Curriculum Authority, OFSTED, LEAs, the Teacher Training Agency, research and training institutions, the range of other INSET providers, school-based development programs, and so on. The program outlined above would have implications for all of them, although it would be for government to give a lead. It would be premature and out of order for us to try to consider their relative roles in such a program, although clearly success would depend on their mutual cooperation.

The main plank of our argument is that standards are raised only by changes put into direct effect by teachers and pupils in classrooms. There is a body of firm evidence that formative assessment is an essential feature of classroom work and that development of it can raise standards. We know of no other way of raising standards for which such a strong prima facie case can be made on the basis of evidence of such large learning gains.

Our education system has been subjected to many far-reaching initiatives which, while taken in reaction to concerns about existing practices, have been based on little evidence about their potential to meet those concerns. In our study of formative assessment there can be seen, for once, firm evidence that indicates clearly a direction for change which could improve standards of learning. Our plea is that national policy will grasp this opportunity and give a lead in this direction.

References

Beaton, A E, Mullis, I V S, Martin, M O, Gonzalez, E J, Kelly, D L & Smith, T A (1996). *Mathematics achievement in the middle school years.* (Boston, MA: Boston College).

Black, P J & Atkin, JM (1996). *Changing the Subject: Innovations in science, mathematics and technology education*, London: Routledge for OECD.

Black, P & Wiliam, D (1998). *Assessment and Classroom Learning. Assessment in Education* 5(1) (in press).

Daws, N & Singh, B (1996). Formative assessment; to what extent is its potential to enhance pupils' science being realized? *School Science Review*, 77 (281), pp 93–100.

Dassa, C, Vazquez-Abad, J & Ajar, D (1993). Formative assessment in a classroom setting: from practice to computer innovations. *The Alberta Journal of Educational Research*, 39(1), pp 111–125.

Daugherty, R (1995). *National Curriculum Assessment. A Review of Policy 1987–1994.* (London: Falmer Press).

DES (1988). *Task Group on Assessment and Testing : A Report* London: Department of Education and Science and the Welsh Office

Fuchs, L S & Fuchs, D (1986). Effects of Systematic Formative Evaluation: a Meta-Analysis. *Exceptional Children*, 53 (3), pp 199–208.

Fuchs, L S, Fuchs, D, Karns, K, Hamlett, C L, Katzaroff, M & Dutka, S (1997). Effects of Task Focused Goals on Low Achieving Students With and Without Learning Disabilities. *American Educational Research Journal*, 34 (3), pp 513–543.

Fullan, M G with Stiegelbauer, S (1991). *The New Meaning of Educational Change.* London: Cassell.

Gipps, C, McCallum, B & Brown, M (1996). Models of teacher assessment among primary school teachers in England. The Curriculum Journal, 7(2), pp 167–183.

Grisay, A (1991). Improving assessment in primary schools: "APER" research reduces failure rates, in: P Weston (Ed) *Assessment of Pupils Achievement: Motivation and School Success*, pp 103–118. (Amsterdam: Swets and Zeitlinger).

Johnston, P, Guice, S, Baker, K, Malone, J & Michelson, N (1995). Assessment of teaching and learning in literature-based classrooms. *Teaching and Teacher Education*, 11 (4), pp 359–371.

OFSTED (1996). *Subjects and Standards. Issues for school development arising from OFSTED inspection findings 1994–5, Key Stages 3 and 4 and post-16.* (London: Her Majesty's Stationery Office)

Perrenoud, P (1991). Towards a pragmatic approach to formative evaluation, in: P Weston (Ed)